IN THE STEPS OF
OUR LORD

F. F. Bruce

KREGEL

PUBLICATIONS

Grand Rapids, MI 49501

Dusk at the Sea of
Galilee

Previous page: An
old doorway in
Bethlehem.

IN THE STEPS OF
OUR LORD

F. F. BRUCE

PHOTOGRAPHS BY TIM DOWLEY AND PETER M. WYART

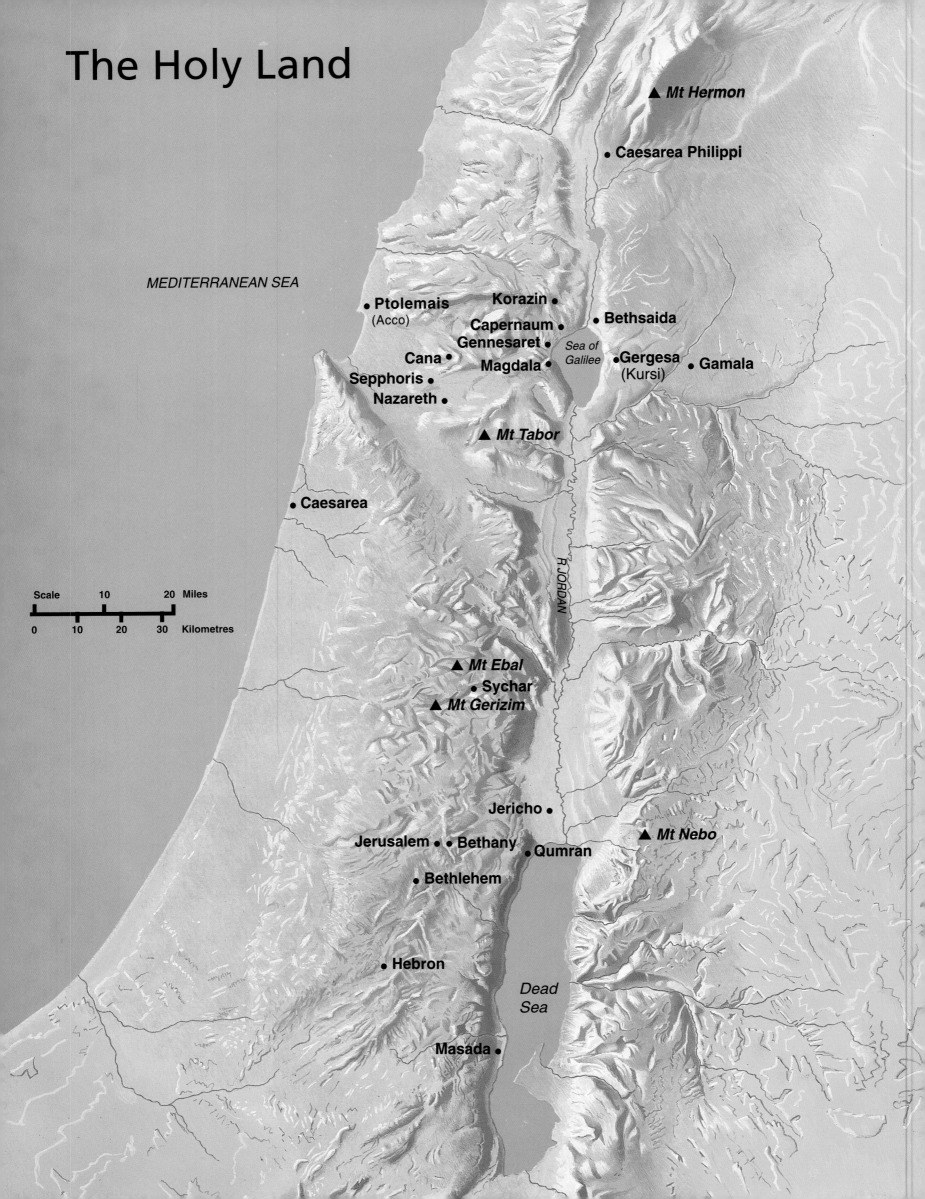

The Holy Land

▲ *Mt Hermon*

● Caesarea Philippi

MEDITERRANEAN SEA

● Ptolemais
(Acco)

● Korazin

● Capernaum

● Bethsaida

Gennesaret

Sea of Galilee

● Cana

Magdala ●

● Gergesa
(Kursi)

● Gamala

● Sepphoris

● Nazareth

▲ *Mt Tabor*

● Caesarea

R. JORDAN

Scale   10   20 Miles

0   10   20   30 Kilometres

▲ *Mt Ebal*

● Sychar

▲ *Mt Gerizim*

Jericho ●

Jerusalem ● ● Bethany

▲ *Mt Nebo*

● Qumran

● Bethlehem

● Hebron

Dead Sea

● Masada

Contents

In the Steps of Our Lord by F. F. Bruce.

Copyright © 1996 by Three's Company/Angus Hudson Ltd.

Published in 1997 by Kregel Publications, a division of Kregel, Inc., P. O. Box 2607, Grand Rapids, MI 49501. Kregel Publications provides trusted, biblical publications for Christian growth and service. Your comments and suggestions are valued.

This text originally appeared as part of *Places They Knew: Jesus and Paul*, (1981) and is used here by kind permission of Scripture Union Publishing.

Designed and created by Three's Company, 5 Dryden Street, London WC2E 9NW

Library of Congress Cataloging-in-Publication Data
Bruce, F. F. (Frederick Fyvie), 1910–1990
  In the steps of Our Lord / F. F. Bruce.
    p. cm.
  Includes index.
  1. Jesus Christ—Biography. 2. Palestine—Pictorial works. I. Title.
    BT301.2.B694   1997
    225.9'1'0222—dc21   97-7913
                            CIP
ISBN 0-8254-2335-x (hardcover)

1 2 3 / 03 02 01 00 99 98 97

Printed in Singapore

A shepherd tends his flock near the ruins of Herod's stronghold at Herodium.

Introduction

A Bedouin encampment in the Judean Hills, near the ancient road from Jerusalem to Jericho.

The people and events described in the Bible were very much down-to-earth; they did not belong to some never-never land above the clouds. Some of the men and women whom we meet in the Bible lived all their lives in the same place; many others travelled widely. Jesus taught for three years only, mainly within Palestine. If we can envisage him in that geographical setting, it helps us to understand many of the things that are recorded about him.

Many features of the Bible lands have changed between those earlier days and our own. The Bedouin tents may still look much as they did in Abraham's time, but the people who live in them today keep in touch with domestic and international news with the aid of transistor radios, which gives them a different outlook on the world. But we can still appreciate the difference between the desert where they live and the cultivated land which adjoins it, or the difference between country life and city life. Egypt's fertility still depends on the Nile, and Syria and the Holy Land still depend on seasonal rainfall for regular harvests.

Human life was controlled by natural conditions in Bible days, and to a large extent it still is. To learn something, therefore, of the places which the Bible characters knew is a great help to seeing their lives and actions in a proper context. The best way to learn, no doubt, is to visit the places ourselves and picture the persons and events associated with them. But if that cannot be done, then photographs and verbal descriptions will do something to fill the gap. Some of the places are still busy centres of human activity; others have been excavated after being covered over for centuries and stand as relics of what once was. Either way, they can teach us something about the Bible story.

F. F. BRUCE

Ancient and modern mingle in the streets of Bethlehem; a street scene near the busy market.

Bethlehem

Bethlehem is first mentioned in the Bible in the story of Jacob's return to his homeland from Mesopotamia. According to Genesis 35:19 Rachel died and was buried 'on the way to Ephrath (that is, Bethlehem)', where her tomb is still shown. This explains 'Rachel weeping for her children' after Herod's massacre of the infants of Bethlehem (Matthew 2:16-18).

The name of the town originally meant 'house of Lahmu' (who was evidently a Canaanite divinity); to the Jews it came to mean 'house of bread'. After the Israelite settlement in Canaan it was allocated to the tribe of Judah. It was the home of the Levite who appears in the story of Micah (Judges 17:7); it was also the home of the ill-fated concubine of another Levite (Judges 19:1). It plays a happier part in the story of Ruth, as the home of Elimelech and Naomi and then as the home of Boaz and Ruth. The book of Ruth ends with a family tree showing how King David was the great-grandson of Boaz and Ruth. It was the fact that David was born and brought up there that gave Bethlehem its fame in Old Testament times. Otherwise it was an unimportant place, not figuring significantly in the history of the monarchy; but in the days when the fortunes of the kingdom of Judah were at a low ebb, the prophet Micah foretold that a ruler would arise from Bethlehem and restore his people's fortunes.

This oracle from Micah 5:2 is quoted in Matthew's nativity narrative, in his account of the visit of the Magi. When they arrived in Jerusalem, asking for the whereabouts of the new-born king of the Jews, they were directed to Herod's palace. Herod summoned the leading rabbis and asked them where the Messiah was to be born. 'In Bethlehem in Judea,' they said, for this was the place indicated by the prophet (Matthew 2:3-6).

Luke, in his nativity narrative, brings Joseph and Mary to Bethlehem immediately before the birth of Jesus because the Roman Emperor, Augustus, had decreed an empire-wide census. The census regulations required that everyone should return to his family home to be enrolled – especially, one supposes, if he or his family owned property there. Joseph, being a member of the family of David, returned to Bethlehem and took his newly-wedded wife with him. There is an impressive contrast, no doubt designed, between the most powerful ruler in the world, issuing his edict from the Palatine in Rome and the child whose birthplace was, as an incidental consequence of

The spot traditionally revered as the site of the birth of Jesus, inside the Church of the Nativity, Bethlehem.

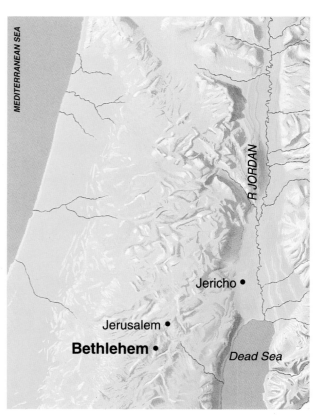

'Let's go to Bethlehem and see this thing that has happened . . .' (Luke 2:15)

'Let's go to Bethlehem and see this thing that has happened . . .' (Luke 2:15)

Opposite: The belfry of the Church of the Nativity, high above Manger Square, Bethlehem.

that edict, in an obscure corner of the empire – a child who was destined nevertheless to wield more extended sovereignty than Augustus ever commanded (Luke 2:1-7).

Matthew and Luke are quite independent of each other in their nativity narratives, but they agree that Jesus was born in Bethlehem, that his mother was a virgin when she conceived him, and that Joseph, her husband and Jesus' legal father, was a descendant of David.

The entrance to the 'birth cave', within the Church of the Nativity, Bethlehem.

In the middle of the second century AD Justin Martyr reports that, since Joseph found nowhere to lodge in Bethlehem itself, he put up in a 'cave' near the village. Justin, as a native of Palestine, may well have known a local tradition that the birthplace of Jesus was a cave used as a stable. Origen of Alexandria, who spent the last twenty-three years of his life (from AD 231 onwards) at Caesarea in Palestine, knew the same tradition. 'At Bethlehem,' he says, 'there is

shown the cave where Jesus was born, and the manger in which he lay wrapped in swaddling bands. Indeed this sight is much mentioned in the places around, even among enemies of the faith: "In this place," they say, "Jesus was born, he who is worshipped and reverenced by the Christians."'

Even today, in the neighbourhood of Bethlehem,

one may occasionally find a cave here and there used (if conveniently close to the owner's house) as a stable. with a manger attached to the wall. It is conceivable, indeed, that such a house might be built near a cave for precisely that reason.

It was probably in recognition of the local tradition known to Justin and Origen, that the Emperor

A coin of Caesar Augustus.

Candles burn in the Church of the Nativity, Bethlehem.

A shepherd leads his flock over the hills near Bethlehem.

The Bethlehem skyline is punctuated by church towers and minarets.

A stall in the busy vegetable market in Bethlehem.

Constantine built over the cave the basilica which was the first Church of the Nativity; it was dedicated in AD 339, two years after Constantine's death. The present Church of the Nativity, on the same site, is basically the work of the Emperor Justinian (AD 527-565). In the course of excavations carried out in 1934 the mosaic floor of Constantine's basilica was brought to light, together with the foundations of its walls.

The angel's announcement to the shepherds of the Saviour's birth (Luke 2:8-18) was early commemorated by a Byzantine church in the area east of the town, called the Shepherds' Fields. In the crypt beneath its ruins Orthodox services are still held.

After his family left Bethlehem there is no record of Jesus' ever visiting the place again. His early association with it was not generally known. Hence, when some of his hearers on one occasion in Jerusalem thought he must be the Messiah, others said that this was impossible, for this man (as everyone knew) was a Galilean, whereas 'the Christ will come from David's family and from Bethlehem, the town where David lived' (John 7:42). John implies that he and his readers share the knowledge of Jesus' actual birthplace, of which most of Jesus' contemporaries were ignorant; this is an instance of what is called 'Johannine irony'.

Bethlehem today is an Arab city, the seat of an Arab university. A large proportion of its Arab population is Christian.

By no means least!

Matthew 2:6, 'But you, Bethlehem, in the land of Judah, are by no means least among the rulers of Judah', quotes Micah 5:2, but with a difference. The oracle in Micah begins, 'But you, Bethlehem Ephrathah, though you are small among the clans of Judah . . . ' The place once described as 'small' has now become 'not least', which means, in effect, 'very great'. It is the birth of Christ there that justifies the change. Note also that Micah continues the oracle beyond the point where Matthew breaks off the quotation: he goes on to say, 'whose origins are from of old, from ancient times.' We might consider how these last words could be true of the child who was born in Bethlehem.

11

Nazareth

Nazareth was a small town in Galilee, about fifteen miles west of the Lake of Galilee and twenty miles east of the Mediterranean, where Joseph and Mary lived and where Jesus was brought up from early childhood. Jesus was therefore commonly known as 'Jesus of Nazareth' or 'Jesus the Nazarene'; and it was probably because of their association with him that his followers, in turn, came to be called Nazarenes.

Nazareth does not appear to have been a place of any significance in antiquity. It is nowhere mentioned in the Old Testament or in pre-Christian Jewish literature. The first reference to it outside Christian literature is in a fragmentary inscription found in the ancient synagogue of Caesarea in 1962, where it is named as one of the places in Galilee where the members of the twenty-four priestly divisions settled after the crushing of the second Jewish revolt against Rome in AD 135. The particular division that settled in Nazareth was that of Happizzez (1 Chronicles 24:15).

Nathanael's question 'Can anything good come from there?' (John 1:46), suggests that Nazareth enjoyed no

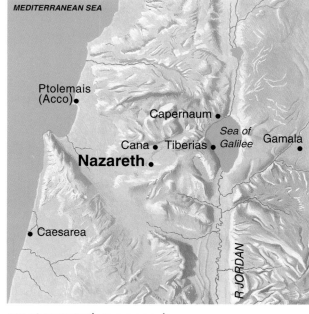

great reputation among its neighbours. In the narrative of Jesus' public ministry Nazareth does not appear in a very favourable light. Mark and Matthew relate that, when Jesus visited the place soon after the beginning of his Galilean ministry, his fellow-townsmen gave him no credence and therefore did not witness any of his mighty works, apart from the healing of a few sick people (Mark 6:1-6; Matthew 13:53-58). Luke adds a summary of his Sabbath-day address in the synagogue, where he took as his text the opening words of Isaiah 61. Jesus explained that his present ministry was to proclaim 'the year of the Lord's favour', implying that he himself was the Spirit-anointed speaker of the passage which he read. The address aroused so much hostility among his hearers that they tried to throw him over 'the brow of the hill on which the town was built' (Luke 4:29) – which is still pointed out as the Mount of Precipitation.

There is an inscribed marble slab in the Louvre in Paris known as the 'Nazareth inscription' because it was sent to France from Nazareth by the collector W. Froehner in 1878. It cannot be established that it was actually set up in Nazareth. It

A sculpture of the holy family, Mary, Joseph and Jesus, at the Church of the Annunciation, Nazareth.

Below: Ancient carpentry tools.

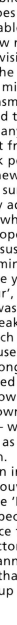

The Greek Catholic Synagogue Church is situated in the market of the old city of Nazareth, and stands beside the synagogue traditionally believed to be where Jesus preached (Matthew 13).

The entrance to the Synagogue Church, Nazareth.

'Nazareth! Can anything good come from there?' (John 1:46)

Opposite: The imposing Church of the Annunciation occupies a prominent site in the centre of the modern town of Nazareth.

contains the text of a Roman imperial edict, commonly ascribed to Claudius (AD 41-54), forbidding the disturbance of tombs. Whether or not this edict (which in any case only restated existing legislation) was a reaction to reports of the empty tomb of Jesus, there is no means of knowing for certain.

Earliest church

Nazareth was a small Jewish village in the early fourth century AD, according to Eusebius of Caesarea. The earliest recorded church in the town is mentioned by a seventh-century writer; it had formerly been a synagogue. Excavations have revealed traces of an earlier church,

Right: The market in Nazareth still bustles with life.

Right: The Church of the Annunciation, built over the site of an earlier Crusader church.

dating from the beginning of the fifth century. A quite magnificent basilica was built there in the twelfth century, during the Crusader domination of Palestine, when Nazareth was the seat of an archbishop. After the expulsion of the Crusaders, Nazareth was destroyed by order of the Sultan Baybars in 1263. It lay derelict for 400 years. Its rehabilitation as a Christian shrine dates from the seventeenth century, when the Franciscans were recognised as guardians of the holy places.

Below: The cave beneath the Church of the Annunciation, dating to before the third century AD.

'God sent the angel Gabriel to Nazareth . . .' (Luke 1:26)

Nazareth is now a city of over 20,000 population, inhabited mainly by Arab Christians. It is indeed the largest Christian city in Israel. The great new Church of the Annunciation, commemorating the incident of Luke 1:26-38, was begun in 1955; the excavating of its foundations provided an opportunity to explore the remains of the Byzantine church which stood on the same site, but also brought evidence to light that the place had been occupied as early as the Middle Bronze Age (around the seventeenth century BC). There can be no certainty that the church actually stands on the site of Mary's house, any more than that St. Joseph's Church stands on the site of Joseph's workshop. The one place in Nazareth which can with confidence be associated with Jesus' family is St. Mary's Well, from which water has been drawn from time immemorial.

The hidden years

Here then in Nazareth Jesus grew up with four younger brothers and an unknown number of sisters. It is precarious to try to fill in the details of those 'hidden years'. But from the high ground above the town a boy like Jesus, interested in the Old Testament writings, could look down on many scenes which figured in the earlier history of his people. To the south stretched the plain of Esdraelon (the valley of Jezreel), which had witnessed a succession of great battles, including Barak's victory over Sisera and good King Josiah's fatal defeat at Megiddo. Beyond the plain of Esdraelon, slightly to the left, was Mount Gilboa, where King Saul had fallen in battle against the Philistines. To the east rose Mount Tabor, 1843 feet (562 metres) high, later to be the traditional (but doubtful) site of the Transfiguration. South-west of Tabor lies the small town of Nain, where Jesus was to restore a widow's son to life as he was being carried out of the town to be buried (Luke 7:11-17). Two or three miles beyond Nain was Shunem, where Elisha's generous hostess had lived (2 Kings 4:8). About nine miles north-east of Nazareth was Cana (if it is to be identified with the modern Khirbet Qana), the home of Nathanael (John 21:2), where Jesus was to perform his 'beginning of miracles' by turning water into wine (John 2:1-11).

Above: Houses built on the hillside of Nazareth.

Off the beaten track

Nazareth lay off the beaten track, but the road from the lake of Galilee to Ptolemais (Acco) ran a few miles to the north, while the great 'Way of the Sea' from Damascus and farther north passed by not far to the south, leading to the Mediterranean coast

Right: Mary's Well, Nazareth.

Left: The Mount of Precipitation, Nazareth, from which it is believed the angry inhabitants attempted to throw Jesus after his synagogue sermon.

Below: An ancient carpenter's tool.

and so south to Egypt. Along it, in both directions, moved trading caravans and detachments of soldiers. Galilee at that time was part of the tetrarchy of Herod Antipas, youngest son of the late Herod the Great, and not a Roman province (as Judea was); so any Roman soldiers seen in Galilee would be seconded to his service. But Herod Antipas ruled by grace of the Romans, and the Roman presence was never far from people's thoughts, even in Galilee.

When Jesus was about nine years old, everyone was talking about the rebellion in Judea led by Judas, a Galilean from Gamala, east of the lake. (In popular usage the term Galilee took in some territory east of the lake as well as the region to the west.) Judas and his followers raised the standard of revolt in AD 6 against Roman control of Judea and the obligation on its inhabitants to pay tribute to the emperor. The rising was crushed, and Judas perished (Acts 5:37), but his ideals lived on and found

fresh champions from time to time.

The people of Nazareth, like the other Galileans, did not have to pay taxes to the emperor, but the issue which involved the Judeans must have been a matter of concern to many of them. Thoughtful boys in Nazareth must have discussed these matters and found their sympathies deeply engaged.

What did Jesus think? We know what he thought in manhood when he answered the question put to him in the temple precincts in Jerusalem: 'Is it right to pay taxes to Caesar or not?' (Mark 12:14).

'Can anything good come out of Nazareth?'

'Nazareth! Can anything good come from there?' (John 1:46) asked Nathanael. If this was a popular saying in that part of Galilee, there may have been some ground for it. There are people who will allow such a piece of proverbial wisdom to prejudice them against entertaining the possibility that there could be an exception to the rule.

Nathanael, happily, did not allow his mind to be prejudiced. He responded readily enough to Philip's invitation 'Come and see', and found that the greatest imaginable good came from such an unlikely place as Nazareth. A willingness to test the evidence for oneself is a sovereign remedy against prejudice.

Galilee

Opposite: A clear day on the edge of the Lake of Galilee.

The Lake (or Sea) of Galilee is a pear-shaped stretch of fresh water into which the Jordan flows from the north and out of which it flows towards the south. It is about thirteen miles (twenty-one km) long from north to south, and nearly eight miles (thirteen km) across from west to east at its greatest width; it lies 695 feet (212 metres) below Mediterranean sea level and reaches a depth of about 200 feet (sixty-one metres).

Its Old Testament name is the Lake of Kinnereth: this word means 'lyre' and has been thought to refer to the shape of the lake, which can easily be seen in its entirety from the higher ground around it. If that is so, then the city of Kinnereth, mentioned in Deuteronomy 3:17 and elsewhere, must take its name from the lake; but if the lake takes its name from the city, the 'lyre-shape' explanation must be given up. In the New Testament it is called not only the Sea Galilee but the Lake of Gennesaret (Luke 5:1), from the fertile plain on its north-west side (modern Ginossar), and the Sea of Tiberias (John 6:1; 21:1), from the city which Herod Antipas built on its western shore about AD 22.

Much of Jesus' public ministry took place around the shores of the lake. One can still be impressed by the acoustic properties of some

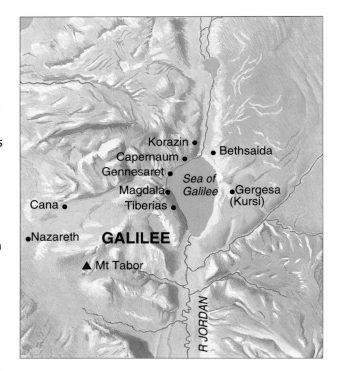

A sculpture of Jesus healing, outside the Church of the Primacy of St. Peter, beside the Lake of Galilee.

of the places from which he taught, whether from the slopes of the rising hill-country to the west (the Mount of the Beatitudes) or from a boat pushed a little way out to sea near Capernaum, from which the people on land could hear him as in a natural amphitheatre. Storms such as those described in the Gospel story still blow up suddenly, when currents of air from the west, passing through the Arbel valley, are sucked down in vortices over the lake.

In Jesus' time the territory west of the lake was ruled by Herod Antipas, tetrarch of Galilee from 4 BC to his deposition in AD 39. Herod's new capital of Tiberias (called after his patron, the Roman Emperor Tiberius) is not said to have been visited by Jesus. In fact, for a long time Jews tended to avoid it, regarding it as ceremonially unclean because it was built on the site of a cemetery. It may have been in his palace at Tiberias that Herod's macabre birthday party was held (Mark 6:21). If so, the messenger who carried the order for John the Baptist's execution had a long way to travel, for Josephus tells us that John was imprisoned and

Fishing boats and tour boats moored at Ein Gev, on the eastern shore of the Lake of Galilee.

put to death in Herod's Transjordan fortress of Machaerus. Josephus is probably right: John was active in the lower Jordan valley, including 'Bethany on the other side of the Jordan' (John 1:28), which lay in Herod's territory of Perea. Before he built Tiberias, Herod lived in Sepphoris, four miles north-west of Nazareth. Rumours of goings-on at his court must have been current in Nazareth, and when some of Jesus' parables were set in royal courts his hearers would have a fair picture of the scene in their mind's eye.

East of the lake the ruler was Herod's brother, Philip the tetrarch (mentioned in Luke 3:1), whose capital was Caesarea Philippi. Philip's territory was untroubled by the tension that made Herod Antipas so suspicious and cunning – it was not for nothing that Jesus called Antipas 'that fox' (Luke 13:32). When Antipas' interest in Jesus became too keen, it was easy to avoid his attention by crossing to the other side of the lake.

A mosaic of loaves and fishes, in front of the altar of the Church of the Multiplication of the Loaves and Fishes, near Capernaum.

The modern visitor finds it difficult to envisage the thriving towns which surrounded the lake in Jesus' day. The lake teemed with fish, which provided a living for many of the inhabitants of those towns. The fish they caught were not only sent to other parts of Palestine and Transjordan, but salted and exported to other lands. Magdala, between Capernaum and Tiberias, was given the Greek name of Tarichaeae, because of the salt fish (*tarichos* in Greek) which it exported. It was the home of Mary Magdalene. Capernaum, which Jesus chose as his headquarters during his ministry in Galilee, is mentioned alongside Korazin and Bethsaida in Matthew 11:20-24 and Luke 10:13-15. Doom is pronounced on all three because, although they had witnessed so many of Jesus' mighty works, they refused to repent.

'Woe to you, Korazin! Woe to you, Bethsaida!' (Mathew 11:21)

Korazin, two and a half miles north of Capernaum, was destroyed at the time of the second Jewish revolt against Rome (AD 132-135) but was rebuilt and remained a flourishing city for some generations, extending to an area of about twelve acres (nearly five hectares). By the time of Eusebius, however (about AD 330), it lay in ruins. It was well supplied with water. The buildings, including the synagogue, were of the local black basalt. The synagogue, many of whose walls still stand, occupied an area of about seventy by fifty feet (about twenty-one by fifteen metres). It was supported by pillars and pilasters whose capitals and cases represented a variety of Greek orders. It was richly decorated with floral designs enclosing human and animal figures, which suggest that its builders and sponsors did not take the second commandment too literally. One of the most interesting pieces of furniture in the synagogue, belonging to the third century AD, was 'Moses' seat' (compare Matthew 23:2), from which the law was read or expounded; it was an armchair of black basalt, decorated with a rosette on the back. Many Jewish houses of the same period have also been excavated, together with water reservoirs and a ritual bath.

Dusk at the mooring place at Ein Gev.

The sun sets over the Lake of Galilee.

The black basalt Church of the Primacy of St. Peter, built over a flat rock known to early pilgirms as Christ's Table.

Bethsaida, which simply means 'Fishertown', lay a little way east of the point where the Jordan enters the lake from the north. Philip the tetrarch enlarged it and changed its name to Julias, in honour of Julia, daughter of the Emperor Augustus. (This must have been not later than 2 BC, for in that year Julia fell into disgrace and was exiled.) It was the original home of Peter and Andrew, and also of Philip the apostle, according to John 1:44. In its neighbourhood the feeding of the five thousand most probably took place. (The traditional site of the feeding, at Tabgha, south-west of Capernaum, is difficult to accept.) Mark also records the healing of a blind man at Bethsaida (Mark 8:22-26).

If one continues round the lake in a clockwise direction, one comes to a place on the east shore called Kursi or Kersa, directly across from Magdala. It is fairly certainly here that the healing of the man possessed by the legion of demons took place. It is the

one point on the east side the lake where the steep hills come right down almost to the water's edge. The modern name preserves the ancient Gerasa or (better) Gergesa. There was a much more important Gerasa (modern Jerash) over forty miles (sixty-five km) to the south, on the main north-south road through Trans-jordan but that

had nothing to do with the place on the lakeside. If the region is called 'the region of the Gadarenes' (Matthew 8:28) that may be because the city of Gadara (modern Umm Qeis), nearly seven miles (about eleven km) south-east of the lake and separated from by the deep Yarmuk gorge, had property around here. The presence of a large

The modern Church of the Sermon on the Mount, on the hill now known as the Mount of the Beatitudes, overlooking the Lake of Galilee.

Left: Fertile hills north of the Lake of Galilee.

The sun sets over the choppy waters of the Lake of Galilee.

herd of pigs in the vicinity is sufficient indication that the local people were Gentiles.

When the demon-possessed man was cured, he 'went away and began to tell in the Decapolis how much Jesus had done for him' (Mark 5:20). The Decapolis was a league of ten cities, the most northerly of which was Damascus and the most southerly Philadelphia (Amman); it included Gadara and Gerasa (Jerash). All but one of these cities – Scythopolis (Beth-shean) – lay east of the Jordan valley. The term Decapolis may also denote, more generally, the area in which the ten cities lay – quite an extensive mission-field for the grateful man. Why did Jesus encourage him to spread the news of his recovery, whereas west of the lake he usually warned those whom he healed to keep quiet about it? Probably because the Decapolis was a Gentile area, where there was no danger of the revolutionary excitement that was always liable to break out among the Jews of Galilee.

Fishers of men

It was by the 'Sea of Galilee' that Jesus called Simon Peter and Andrew from their fishing and promised to make them 'fishers of men' (Matthew 4:18-20). It was by the same sea that, according to John 21:15-17, he appeared to his disciples in resurrection and recommissioned Peter to feed his sheep. The catching of fish may describe the work of an evangelist, but the feeding of sheep is the work of a pastor: both are essential. So, at the beginning of the ministry of the earthly Christ and at the beginning of the ministry of the risen Christ the Galilean lakeside provides an appropriate setting.

Capernaum

Capernaum was the town on the western shore of the Lake of Galilee where Jesus made his headquarters when he came into Galilee preaching the good news of the kingdom of God after John the Baptist's imprisonment. Here Simon Peter and Andrew lived (Mark 1:29) although, according to John 1:44, they originally came from Bethsaida. Jesus preached in the synagogue of Capernaum one sabbath day early in his Galilean ministry and impressed the congregation by the authority with which he expelled a demon from a possessed man. 'That evening, after sunset', he cured a great number of sick people, so that his fame spread throughout the town and into the surrounding countryside (Mark 1:21-45).

It was in Capernaum, too, that he cured the paralysed man who was let down by his friends through a hole in the roof, and it was on the quayside of the town that he called Matthew-Levi to leave the collecting of taxes and follow him as a disciple (Mark 2:1-14). 'It was here, on the harbour steps at Capernaum,' wrote Dr. W. M. Christie, 'that Peter learned to swear. When he landed his fish, there sat Matthew, the publican, demanding his tax of one from every five . . . And if ever cursing was justifiable, it was when such as Peter the fisherman cursed Matthew the publican.'

It was in Capernaum that the centurion lived whose servant was cured by an authoritative word from Jesus spoken at a distance. This centurion is said to have built the local synagogue as a

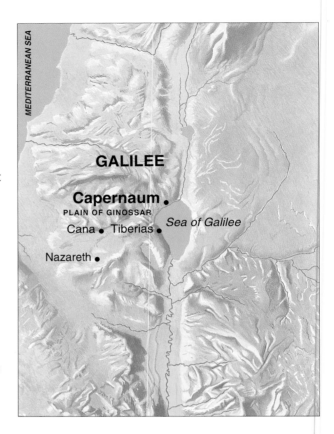

GALILEE

Capernaum
PLAIN OF GINOSSAR
Cana • Tiberias • *Sea of Galilee*

Nazareth •

MEDITERRANEAN SEA

Reconstructed remains of an early synagogue at Capernaum, possibly built on the site of the building which Jesus knew.

Left: The gardens at Capernaum are tended carefully by the Franciscans.

Above: A mosaic of a small boat, Capernaum.

token of his friendship for the Jewish community. He was presumably a non-commissioned officer from the Roman army seconded to the service of Herod Antipas. The relation of this healing narrative (Matthew 8:5-13; Luke 7:2-10) to that of the healing of the official's son in Capernaum by a word spoken in Cana (John 4:46-54) is debated; that official was also in Herod's service, but not necessarily a member of his armed forces.

John tells us that it was in the Capernaum synagogue that Jesus delivered his discourse on the bread of life after the feeding of the five thousand (John 6:59).

But as time went on Jesus was no longer so welcome as a preacher in the synagogue as he was at the beginning of his ministry. In particular, his insistence on healing people there on the Sabbath, even while the service was in progress, was felt by the synagogue authorities to be intolerable. So the mountain slope and the lakeside had to serve as his auditoria, but there he was heard by greater crowds than could be accommodated in the synagogue.

It was to Capernaum that Jesus and the disciples repeatedly returned from journeys throughout Galilee. Here, probably, he raised Jairus' daughter from her deathbed (Mark 5:21-43); here he taught his disciples the lesson of humility by the example of the child whom he set in their midst (Mark 9:33-37); here he discussed with Peter the propriety of paying the Temple tax and sent him to catch a fish to pay it for both of them (Matthew 17:24-27).

Capernaum, or Kefar Nahum, means 'the village of Nahum' – but it is not known which Nahum is meant. Josephus says that its hinterland was very fertile; he records how its inhabitants played an active part in the revolt against Rome which broke out in AD 66. It is mentioned also in rabbinical literature. But later its true location was forgotten for centuries. Well into the twentieth century two sites competed for identification with Capernaum, both on the north-west shore of the lake – Khirbet el-Minyeh – at the

Opposite: Two columns from the reconstructed Capernaum synagogue.

Above: Masonry found at Capernaum includes stones with symbols of great significance to Jewish people, including the Ark of the Covenant, the Menorah, the Star of David and grapes.

entrance to the Plain of Ginossar, and Tell Hum (as it is called by the Arabs), four miles (six and a half km) to the north-east and three miles (nearly five km) west of the place where the Jordan enters the lake. The Tell Hum identification has won the day, and rightly so: on Israeli road-signs and official maps Tell Hum is called Capernaum. The ruins of the town extend for a mile (about two km) along the shore. The Arabic name Tell Hum does not imply (as place-names introduced by the element *tell* normally do) that there is a mound on the site covering layers of successive settlements. It is probably a corruption of Telonion, a name which was given to the place in the Middle Ages – and *telonion* is simply the Greek word for 'tax office' in the story of Matthew-Levi's call to discipleship (Mark 2:14).

Excavations have been carried out on the site for many years, especially since 1894, when it was bought by

the Franciscans and fenced round for security. The most imposing landmark on the site is the magnificently ornamented two-storey synagogue of white limestone, some sixty-five feet (twenty metres) long, partly restored by the Franciscans. Its style of

architecture and decoration, together with dedicatory inscriptions, suggest that it was built about the beginning of the third century AD. It was not the synagogue in which Jesus taught, though it may have been built on the site of that earlier one.

Below: An ancient olive press, made of black basalt, at Capernaum.

A half shekel coin.

Part of the excavated site of ancient Capernaum.

The Greek Orthodox monastery near the site of ancient Capernaum.

An octagonal church-building, with a fine mosaic floor, dates from the middle of the fifteenth century. Its builders believed that it covered the site of Peter's house. This building replaced an earlier one on the site which was seen by the pilgrim Egeria in AD 383. 'In Capernaum,' she says, 'the house of the prince of the apostles has been made into a church, with its original walls still standing.' And excavations beneath the foundations of the octagonal church have uncovered the remains of a modest house, one room of which was apparently used as a chapel and bears signs of early Christian veneration.

The abandonment of the site of the town from the seventh century onwards may be thought to provide a commentary on Jesus' sad words: 'And you, Capernaum, will you be lifted up to the skies? No, you will go down to the depth. If the miracles that were performed in you had been performed in Sodom, it would have remained to this day' (Matthew 11:23; compare Luke 10:15).

Capernaum and the Gentiles

Leaving Nazareth, Jesus 'went and lived in Capernaum, which was by the lake' (Matthew 4:13), and this is said to fulfil Isaiah's promise of blessing for 'Galilee of the Gentiles' (Isaiah 9:1). Not many Gentiles were directly blessed during Jesus' Galilean ministry: so far as Capernaum is concerned, the only exceptions recorded are the centurion and his servant (Matthew 8:5-13). But it was in Galilee, on an unnamed mountain, that the risen Christ appeared to the apostles and commissioned them to 'make disciples of all nations' (Matthew 28:19) – that is to say, Gentiles. Perhaps, then, Matthew reckoned that Isaiah's prophecy stretched forward into the world-wide mission which followed the resurrection of Christ.

Caesarea Philippi

Caesarea Philippi figures only once in the gospel story. At the end of his Galilean ministry Jesus took his disciples away into the territory east and north of Galilee, and came with them 'to the villages around Caesarea Philippi' (Mark 8:27). He is not said to have visited the city of Caesarea Philippi itself: its 'villages' stood in the surrounding 'region' (Matthew 16:13), which it controlled. It was in this district that he asked his disciples who people said he was and then asked them what account they themselves had to give of him.

Caesarea Philippi is the modern Banyas, standing on a terrace about 1,150 feet (350 metres) high, at the foot of Mount Hermon. Mount Hermon rises on the north-east to a height of 9,100 feet (2,774 metres). The Nahr Banyas, one of the principal sources of the Jordan, springs from a cave in the cliff-face here, and waters the whole terrace.

The spot was probably frequented as a shrine in antiquity. It is widely thought to have been the place mentioned in Joshua 11:17 as the northernmost limit of Joshua's conquest: 'Baal-gad in the valley of Lebanon below Mount Hermon.' Baal-gad means 'lord of fortune' and was presumably the divinity worshipped at the place called by his name. But this is speculation – we are on firmer footing when we come to the Greek period.

Shortly after the conquest of this area by Alexander the Great (332 BC), the Greeks dedicated the grotto from which Nahr Banyas springs 'to Pan and the Nymphs' (as we know from an inscription on the rock-face). From its dedication to Pan the shrine was called the Paneion and the city and district were called Paneias. Here, in 200 BC, a decisive battle was fought between the Seleucid king of Syria and the Ptolemaic king of Egypt.

As a result of this battle, which the Seleucid king won, Lebanon and Palestine became part of his kingdom and were henceforth ruled from Antioch, instead of being ruled from Alexandria, the capital of the Ptolemaic kingdom, as they had been for over a century. This battle, between 'the king of the north' (Antiochus III) and 'the king of the south' (Ptolemy V), is mentioned in Daniel 11:15-16, where the 'fortified city' is Paneias and the 'Beautiful Land' is Palestine – or perhaps, more strictly, Judea.

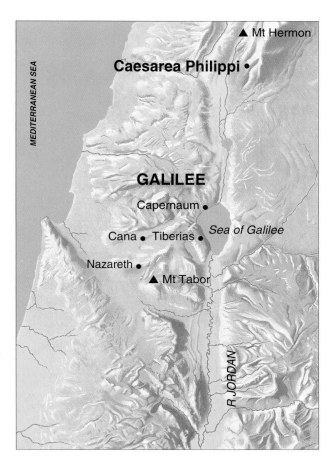

The snow-capped heights of Mount Hermon, in the far north of Israel.

Niches in the cliff face at Banyas were cut to receive statues during the Graeco-Roman period.

In 64 and 63 BC the district of Paneias, with the whole of Syria and Palestine, came under the control of Rome. In due course Paneias was added by the Emperor Augustus to the kingdom of Herod the Great, who acknowledged the gift by erecting a marble temple in honour of Augustus. When Herod died in 4 BC, Paneias was included in the territory east and north of the lake of Galilee bequeathed to his son Philip the tetrarch (mentioned in Luke 3:1). Philip refounded Paneias as the capital of his tetrarchy and, by way of compliment to Augustus, who had confirmed Herod's bequest, renamed the city Caesarea. To distinguish it from Caesarea on the Mediterranean seaboard of Palestine (founded by Herod several years before and named in honour of the same emperor), this was commonly known as 'Philip's Caesarea', in Latin, Caesarea Philippi. Philip was the most moderate of all Herod's sons who succeeded to parts of his kingdom – partly, no doubt, because his subjects were mainly Gentiles. When tension mounted in Galilee, and it became expedient for Jesus and his disciples to avoid the

attention of Herod Antipas, it was easy for them to get into a boat and cross the lake into Philip's territory. Twenty years after Philip's death (in AD 34), his grand-nephew the younger Agrippa (whom Paul could not altogether persuade to be a Christian) received Caesarea Philippi as the capital of his kingdom (which covered more or less the former tetrarchy of Philip). He gave it the new name Neronias, as a compliment,

this time, to the Emperor Nero. This new name did not last very long. Later, with the recession of Greek and Roman influence in those parts, and the reassertion of Semitic dominance, the name Caesarea Philippi also fell into disuse. The name which survived was Paneias, originally a Greek name, but altered in time to Banyas because of the Arabs' difficulty in pronouncing the 'p' sound.

Waterfall at Banyas. The stream which arises from a spring at Banyas is a principal source of the river Jordan.

An Arab woman bakes unleavened bread over an open fire at Banyas.

An Arab family picnic in the shade of trees at the beautiful park at Banyas.

Not much of the ancient architecture of Caesarea Philippi remains intact: hewn stones are scattered all over the site.

Josephus relates a story intended to prove that the spring of Banyas was fed by an underground stream from the circular Lake Phiale (the modern Birket Ram), seven miles (just over eleven km) to the east. But there is no connection between them: Lake Phiale is the water-filled crater of an extinct volcano.

The events in the district of Caesarea Philippi marked the end of one phase in Jesus' ministry and the beginning of a new one. When, in response to his question, 'But who do you say I am?' (Mark 8:29), Peter confessed him to be the Messiah, he began to tell his disciples, to their shocked bewilderment, that this involved his suffering and death. His Galilean ministry had now come to an end, and soon afterwards, for the last time, he set out with them on the southward road to Judea and Jerusalem.

'Who do people say I am?'

Jesus' question, 'Who do people say I am?' (Mark 8:27-30) receives an even greater variety of answers today than it did when it was first put to the disciples in the neighbour-hood of Caesarea Philippi. One interesting point about this question (and still more so about the personal question which followed, 'But what about you? . . .Who do you say I am?') is that the answer tells us much more about the person who gives it than it tells us about Jesus. 'Indeed, it may be said of all theological schools of thought: "By their Lives of Jesus ye shall know them"' (T.W. Manson).

Sychar

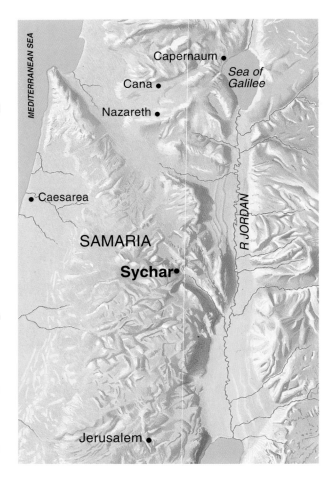

Sychar, near which Jesus held his conversation with the woman at the well, is described in John 4:5 as 'a town in Samaria . . . near the plot of ground Jacob had given to his son Joseph'. The piece of land which Jacob gave to Joseph is mentioned in Genesis 48:22, where Jacob on his deathbed says to Joseph, 'to you, as one who is over your brothers, I give the ridge of land (Hebrew *shechem*, 'shoulder') I took from the Amorites with my sword and my bow'. This military exploit is otherwise unchronicled in the Old Testament: it is hardly to be identified with Simeon and Levi's murderous attack on the people of Shechem (Genesis 34:25-31).

When the Israelites settled in central Canaan, they buried Joseph's bones, which they had brought from Egypt, 'at Shechem in the tract of land that Jacob bought for a hundred pieces of silver' (or, as the New English Bible has it, 'a hundred sheep'; compare Genesis 33:19) from the sons of Hamor, the father of Shechem. This became an inheritance of Joseph's descendants (Joshua 24: 32). The tomb of Joseph is still pointed out; it is covered with a dome, like many other 'welis', or monuments of holy men, in the Islamic world.

About 325 yards (300 metres) south-east of Joseph's tomb lies Jacob's well. As is usual with wells, springs and pools mentioned in the Bible, the authenticity of this well is as certain as anything of the

The town of Nablus viewed from Mount Gerizim.

kind can reasonably be. Although the Samaritan woman said that 'our father Jacob. . . gave us the well and drank from it himself, as did also his sons, and his flocks and herds' (John 4: 12), there is no account of this in the Genesis narrative. The woman was probably repeating an ancient and reliable local tradition.

The pilgrim from Bordeaux who visited the place in AD 333 notes that 'some plane trees are there, planted by Jacob, and there is a bath which receives its water from this well.' Half a century later, a church building stood over the well; it was seen probably by the pilgrim Egeria in AD 381, and certainly by Jerome about AD 390. Seven centuries later the Crusaders built another church on the spot. Both in their turn were destroyed by Muslims. The site is now marked by an unfinished Orthodox church,

The entrance to the site of Jacob's Well, Nablus, believed to be where Jesus met the Samaritan woman (John 4).

begun early in the twentieth century. To approach the well head today one must go down into the crypt of this church; it is no longer

exposed to sun and air, as it was in Jesus' day.

Two different Greek words are used for the well in John's Gospel: one means a well or cistern which is dug out (so as to receive and retain rainwater); the other means a natural spring. Both words are applicable to Jacob's well: it was dug, indeed, but 'is fed by an underground stream, which rarely gives out' (E. E. F. Bishop). The woman spoke truly when she said, 'the well is deep' (John 4:11). Even today it is said to be about 130 feet (forty metres) deep, and it was probably deeper then. Canon H.B. Tristram, a famous Palestinian explorer of the nineteenth century, is said on one occasion to have 'sat thus by the well' about midday and started to read the fourth chapter of John. As he read, he grew drowsy in the heat of the sun and suddenly let his New Testament fall from his hands into the well. (At that time the well was not yet built over.) The book was recovered several years later during an unusually dry winter.

The well stands near the ancient north-south road from Galilee to Judea through

Arab women busy in the fields, near Nablus.

The modern town of Nablus, situated between Mount Ebal and Mount Gerizim.

central Palestine. It was natural that Jesus, weary and hot with his journey, should turn off the road and sit at the well head, asking the favour of a drink from the first person who came to draw water. He does not appear to have troubled about the risk of his incurring ritual pollution: as the New English Bible correctly renders the last clause of John 4:9, 'Jews and Samaritans . . . do not use vessels in common'. But that he should engage in serious religious discussion with a woman, and a Samaritan woman at that, surprised his disciples when they rejoined him.

The water in the well is still beautifully refreshing, even if it remains true that 'everyone who drinks this water will be thirsty again' (John 4:13).

'This mountain' on which, as the woman said, 'our fathers worshipped' (John 4:20), is Mount Gerizim, which rises on the south to a height of 2,900 feet (884 metres) above Mediterranean sea level and 700 feet (213 metres) above the pass lying between it and Mount Ebal on the north. (Mount Ebal is rather higher, about 3,077 feet [938 metres] above Mediterranean sea level.) Gerizim is still to the Samaritan community the holiest place on earth, chosen by the Lord out of all the tribes of Israel 'to put his Name there for his dwelling' (Deuteronomy 12:5).

The site of the 'city' of Sychar is disputed. Two miles (rather more than three km) to the west is the modern city of Nablus, perpetuating the name of Flavia Neapolis, founded by the Roman Emperor Vespasian in AD 72. Immediately to the south of Joseph's tomb is Tell Balatah, marking the site of the Old Testament Shechem. The Old Syriac version of the Gospels translated Sychar as Shechem, and Jerome thought that Sychar was a corruption of Shechem; but the Greek text makes a clear distinction between Sychar and Shechem

Mount Ebal viewed from Mount Gerizim.

(*Sychem* in Greek). Sychar has been commonly identified with the village of 'Askar, less than a mile (about one and a half km) north of Jacob's well. This identification may be correct, although no reliance should be placed on the similarity of name, for *'askar* is an Arabic term for a military camp, and would not be known in Palestine before the Arab conquest of the seventh century AD. But three hundred years and more before the Arab conquest Eusebius of Caesarea (about AD 325) and the Bordeaux pilgrim (AD 333) distinguish Sychar from the ruined Shechem and the inhabited Neapolis. The Bordeaux pilgrim says that Sychar lay a Roman mile distant from Shechem. It appears, then, that the name Sychar was known in the fourth century and is quite independent of the Arabic word *'askar*, although that Arabic word was later given as a name to the place earlier known as Sychar.

The Talmud twice mentions a spring called 'Ain Soker, which may be identical with the plentiful fountain still existing in 'Askar. If so, the Hebrew name of Sychar was Soker. (Some centuries before that, about 100 BC, the *Book of Jubilees* mentions a place in the Shechem area called Sakir.) If the town from which the woman came occupied the site of modern 'Askar, she would have passed the fountain 'Ain Soker and also crossed a stream on her way to Jacob's well; but perhaps she preferred not to join her neighbours in drawing water from the sources which they frequented.

Only mentioned once

John 4:5 is the only place in the Bible where Sychar is mentioned, but the conversation at the wellhead has immortalised the name of the place. A nineteenth-century devotional writer, John Gifford Bellett, is said to have died with the words on his lips: 'Oh, the Man of Sychar!' That such a rare placename should be used to supply our Lord with a very fitting designation bears witness to the impact of this chapter.

Had we been in Jesus' place we should probably have told the Samaritan woman that she needed to be born again (John 4:20-26), and discussed the nature of true worship with Nicodemus. Why did he do it the other way round ?

'Others have done the hard work' (John 4:38). Who were they? Aenon and Salim, where John the Baptist and his disciples ministered for a short time (John 3:23), were in the same region as Sychar. Perhaps it was into their labour that the disciples of Jesus had now entered.

Jericho

Jericho plays a notable part in the gospel narrative of Jesus' last journey to Jerusalem. It is here that he gave blind Bartimaeus the power to see, here too that he invited himself to be a guest in the house of Zacchaeus, the chief tax-collector of the district (Luke 18:35–19:10).

No doubt Jesus had visited Jericho on several earlier occasions. The traditional site of his baptism in the Jordan is about five miles (eight km) to the east; Mount Quarantana, the traditional place of his forty days' fast and temptation, rises to the north-west (due west of Tell es-Sultan). The old road down from Jerusalem (2,500 feet (762 metres) above Mediterranean sea level) to Jericho (820 feet – 250 metres – below), descending well over 3,500 feet (1067 metres) in some fifteen miles (four and a half km), follows the course of the Wadi Qilt; this road was the scene of the 'mugging' which features in the parable of the good Samaritan. The courtyard of the Inn of the Good

Samaritan marks the supposed site of the place where the injured man was lodged and tended (Luke 10:30-35).

The Jericho that Jesus knew lay nearly two miles (about three km) south of the Old Testament Jericho. The site of Old Testament Jericho – the city destroyed by Joshua and rebuilt 400 years later by Hiel of Bethel (1 Kings 16:34) – is marked by the mound called Tell es-Sultan, near Elisha's fountain ('Ain es-Sultan), the perennial spring whose plentiful water-supply of 1,000 gallons (4,546 litres) a minute irrigates the whole surrounding countryside and makes it a place of palm-trees, gardens and plantations.

New Testament Jericho, represented by the ruins called Tulul Abu el-'Alayiq, had its beginnings in the period following the return from the Babylonian exile. The Hellenistic rulers erected a fortress here to guard the road from the Jordan to Jerusalem. Bacchides, a general of the Seleucid kingdom who waged war

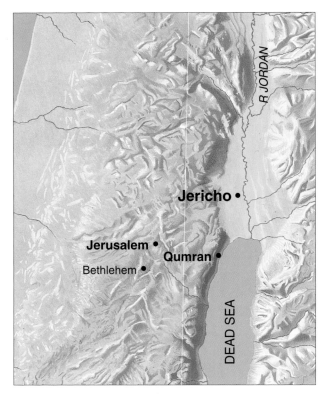

with Judas Maccabaeus, added further fortifications about 160 BC, and the early Hasmonaean rulers continued these operations. It was at Jericho that Simon the Hasmonaean high priest, last surviving brother of Judas Maccabaeus, was assassinated by his son-in-law in 134 BC.

'A man was going down from Jerusalem to Jericho . . .' (Luke 10:30)

A corner of the ruins of the Hasmonean Palace, part of the Herodian city of Jericho.

The excavated site of ancient Jericho (Tel Jericho), include a stone tower constructed c 7000 BC.

The importance of Jericho economically as well as strategically was, if anything, enhanced under the Roman occupation, from 63 BC onwards. The presence of a chief tax-collector in Jericho in the time of Jesus is not at all surprising: the city commanded the main road from Transjordan into Judea. Herod the Great (37–4 BC) constructed a series of fortresses around the area to protect it, and augmented its water-supply by a system of aqueducts bringing water from other sources than Elisha's fountain (always the principal source). He built a new city on both sides of the Wadi Qilt, after the style of contemporary Italian cities, in which lavish use was made of *opus reticulatum* (in which lozenge-shaped pieces of stone were set in concrete). Herodian Jericho, in fact, resembled a more extensive Pompeii. It contained public buildings, amphitheatre, hippodrome, gymnasium or palaestra (wrestling arena), parks, gardens, pools and villas, and (most impressive of

An Arab shepherd grazes his flock near Tel Jericho.

A coin dating from the Jewish revolt.

all) a luxuriously appointed winter palace. It was here that Herod died in 4 BC.

Jericho suffered damage by fire in the disorders which broke out after Herod's death, but was soon restored by his son Archelaus. It was taken, but not destroyed, by Vespasian in AD 68, when, as commander-in-chief of the Roman forces in Judea, he was engaged in suppressing the Jewish revolt. It has been thought that about the same time some of his troops attacked and destroyed the Essene settlement at Qumran, about eight miles (nearly thirteen km) south of Jericho, on the north-west shore of the Dead Sea. Vespasian, having captured Jericho, stationed large bodies of soldiers there in preparation for his attack on Jerusalem. When the second Jewish revolt against the Romans broke out in AD 132, under the leadership of Bar-kokhba, Jericho was again fortified by the Romans and served as a centre from which insurgent outposts in the wilderness of Judea were reduced.

After the suppression of the revolt in AD 135, the importance of Jericho began to decline. The Bordeaux pilgrim visited the city in AD 333 and was shown the

sycamore tree which Zacchaeus climbed. (Jerome also refers to the sycamore over half a century later; so does Peter the Deacon, of Monte Cassino, who wrote a book on the holy places about 1137, during the period of Crusader rule). Whatever may be thought of the genuine-ness of the sycamore, there is no doubt about Elisha's fountain, which the Bordeaux pilgrim also saw: it is one and a half Roman miles from Roman Jericho, he says, adding that any woman who drinks from it will have children – thanks to Elisha's healing of the water with salt (2 Kings 2:19-22). He was shown the house of Rahab

standing above the spring: whoever showed him this must be given credit at least for knowing that Old Testament Jericho stood in that neighbourhood, some distance from Roman Jericho.

Not long after the Bordeaux pilgrim's visit Roman Jericho was deserted. A new city was founded in Byzantine times about a mile (just over one and a half km) to the east of it; it is on the site of the Byzantine city that modern Jericho stands still, like its Old Testament predecessor, 'the City of Palms' (Deuteronomy 34:3).

City of the curse – or blessing?

Jericho in the Old Testament is the city of the curse – but not invariably so. There was a school of prophets there (2 Kings 2:5), and they do not appear to have been troubled by the thought that they were living on accursed ground. Elisha healed the water of the spring there (2 Kings 2:21), so the blessing of God proved more powerful than

the curse of Joshua 6:26. And when Jesus came to Jericho (Luke 18:35–19:10), nothing but blessing attended his visit: Bartimaeus received his sight and Zacchaeus was made a new man, for, as Jesus proclaimed there of all places, 'the Son of man came to seek and to save the lost' – to turn the curse into a blessing.

Bethany

Bethany is best known in the gospel story as the home of Mary, Martha and Lazarus. Luke does not give us the name of the 'village' where Martha (evidently the older sister) 'opened her home to Jesus', but it must have been Bethany, if John's record is allowed to shed light on Luke's. Here Mary sat at Jesus' feet and listened to his teaching while Martha was busily engaged in preparing a meal for the honoured guest (Luke 10:38-42). Here, later, Lazarus their brother fell ill and died, and was raised to life by Jesus (John 11:1-44). Here Jesus was guest of honour at a meal during Holy Week, 'in the home of . . . Simon the Leper' (Mark 14:3; compare John 12:2), and was anointed with costly nard by a woman whom John identifies as Mary. Later, after he was raised from the dead, Jesus led his disciples out 'to the vicinity of Bethany' and took his leave of them (Luke 24:50, 51; compare Acts 1:9-12).

Bethany lies on the eastern slope of the Mount of Olives,

less than two miles (about three km) from Jerusalem (John 11:18). The meaning of the name is uncertain: if it is an abbreviation of Beth-Ananiah (the house of Ananiah), it may be the Ananiah of Nehemiah 11:32. Bethany, as such, first appears in literature in Judith 1:9, where it is mentioned alongside Jerusalem. It was the last staging-post on the road from Jericho to Jerusalem.

The Bordeaux pilgrim visited Bethany in AD 333 and was shown the vault or crypt in which the body of Lazarus was believed to have lain. Eusebius of Caesarea mentions the vault or crypt around the same time. Not long afterwards a church was built over the site, for Egeria saw it in AD 381: she tells how a special service was held there towards the end of Lent, 'six days before the Passover' (compare John 12:1). It is from this church, called the Lazareion (or shrine of Lazarus), that the Muslim name of the village, El-Azariyeh, is derived. The

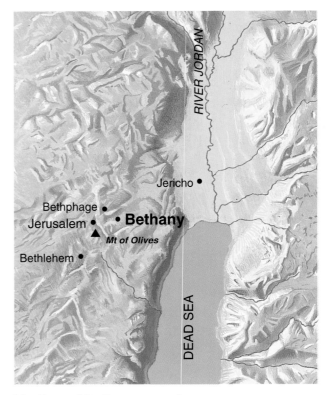

Muslims of Bethany regard Lazarus as a saint. Egeria saw another church half a mile (about one kilometre) on the Jerusalem side of the Lazareion, at the reported spot where Mary met the Lord as he was on his way to the tomb of Lazarus (John 11:29)

The entrance to 'Lazarus' tomb', Bethany.

The impressive modern Franciscan church at Bethany, the fourth on the site to commemorate the resurrection of Lazarus.

Interior of the Franciscan church at Bethany.

– an improbable site, because Jesus on this occasion came to Bethany from the Jordan, not from Jerusalem.

Excavations conducted in Bethany between 1949 and 1953 uncovered remains of four churches, the later ones built over the earlier ones, to the east of the traditional tomb of Lazarus. The earliest of the four may have been the church seen by Egeria. Mosaics from all of them could be distinguished. In their precincts and vicinity were many rock-cut tombs.

The most recent of these four churches was transformed into a mosque, which still stands.

The visitor to Bethany today is shown an opening in the hillside leading into underground chamber traditionally held to be the tomb of Lazarus. Some fifty feet lower down, the modern Franciscan Church of St. Lazarus was built in 1953, on the supposed site of Martha's house. It is beautifully decorated with murals depicting relevant scenes

from the gospel narrative. Some interesting relics are housed in it, including a mosaic from the sixth-century Byzantine church which once stood there, and a Roman inscription bearing witness to the presence nearby of the Tenth (Fretensian) Legion, the military unit which occupied Judea after the fall of Jerusalem in AD 70.

The old road from Bethany to Jerusalem, crossing the summit of the Mount of Olives, passed by Bethphage (meaning 'the place of figs').

Bethany, with (left-right) the Franciscan church, mosque and Greek Orthodox church.

This was the village where the disciples found the donkey ready tethered for Jesus' use and brought it to their master, in accordance with his instructions, so that he might complete his journey to Jerusalem on its back (Mark 11:1-10). It is frequently suggested that the present village of Et-Tur, on the summit, stands where Bethphage stood. This may well be so. The small Franciscan church marking the spot where Jesus is held to have mounted the donkey stands some way down the eastern slope, on the Bethany side of Et-Tur, but Jesus is not said to have mounted the donkey at Bethphage: the disciples brought it from the village to the point which Jesus had reached on his way from Bethany. From this church a procession to Jerusalem starts every Palm Sunday. A similar procession is described by Egeria in AD 384, except that in her day it set out from the church called Eleona (built by the Emperor Constantine on the summit to commemorate the Ascension). The procession, as it moves down the western slope of the hill passes the church called Dominus Flevit ('The

Lord wept'), marking the spot where Jesus came in sight of Jerusalem and wept over it (Luke 19:41). The dome of the church has the shape of a tear-drop, and in front of the little altar within there is a mosaic depicting a hen gathering her chicks under her wings (compare Matthew 23:37).

Bethany – place of rest and blessing

The village is not named in Luke 10:38-42, but comparison with John's record (John 11:1-44) leaves us in no doubt that it was Bethany. Here we are introduced to the two sisters and their respective activities when Jesus visited them: Martha waiting on him and Mary learning from him.

That Jesus is the resurrection and the life is declared in word and shown in action at Bethany.

After the excitement in Jerusalem day by day during Holy Week, Bethany provides welcome rest by night (Mark 11:11).

The supper party at

Bethany provides a setting for the anointing of Jesus (Mark 14:3-9; John 12:1-8). At least one person recognises his royal dignity. The costliness of the ointment is emphasised: nothing but the best is good enough for the King of kings. And when we are tempted to say, 'It could have been sold for more than a year's wages and the money given to the poor,' let us reflect who it was that first said it.

In Luke 24:50,51 Bethany is the scene of the final blessing and parting.

Jerusalem

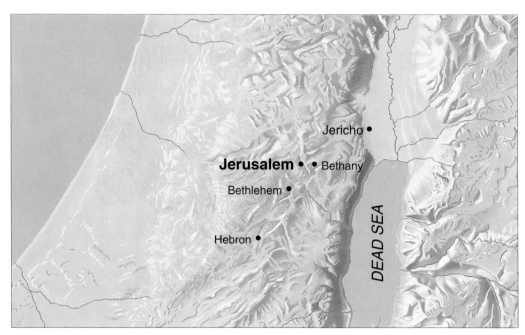

The 'Synoptic Gospels' (Matthew, Mark, Luke) tell of only one visit by Jesus to Jerusalem, the visit during which he was arrested, put on trial and crucified – except for Luke's account of his being taken there in his infancy and later at the age of twelve (Luke 2:22-50). John, on the other hand, tells of several occasions when he visited Jerusalem in the course of his ministry, especially at some of the great feasts of the Jewish year (John 2:13; 5:1; 7:10; 10:22;12:12). It would be surprising if he had not paid repeated visits to Jerusalem, and indeed the Synoptic record suggests that he did visit it several times, when he is reported as addressing the city: 'How often have I longed to gather your children together . . .' (Luke 13:34). Even if, as some think, these words are quoted from a 'wisdom' saying, they would not have been relevant unless they had expressed his own experience.

The Jerusalem that Jesus knew was small in scope but impressive in appearance. Its status as a holy city had been confirmed to it by successive Gentile overlords – Persian, Greek and Roman. Jesus called it 'the city of the Great King' (Matthew 5:35), quoting Psalm 48:2. Whether the psalmist was referring to God or to a king of David's line, there is no doubt that on Jesus' lips 'the Great King' was God. In Jewish belief, Jerusalem was the city which the God of Israel had chosen

The Golden Gate, Jerusalem; by tradition the gate will not be opened until Christ returns.

An Arab visitor to the Dome of the Rock.

'to put his Name there for his dwelling' (Deuteronomy 12:5). By Jesus' day it had changed almost beyond recognition from the city that was hurriedly rebuilt by the impoverished Jews who returned from the Babylonian exile in 539 BC and the following years.

The main quarters of the city, however, remained much as they had been before: they were determined largely by natural features. The city was divided into two parts by the north-south line of the Tyropoeon Valley (the Valley of the Cheesemakers) East of that valley stood the Temple and associated buildings; south of the Temple stood the lower city, the eastern section of which (Ophel) was the original Jerusalem which David captured from the Jebusites and chose as his own capital (2 Samuel 5:6-9). West of the Tyropoeon Valley was the upper city, which does not appear to have been settled so early as the lower city. The south-west quarter was evidently first occupied during the Judean monarchy: it may have been the 'Second Quarter' in which the prophetess Huldah lived about 621 BC (2 Kings 22:14).

Perhaps eighty years after the return from exile, an abortive attempt was made to surround the city with a wall (Ezra 4:12). The building of a wall was actually carried through by Nehemiah, in accordance with the decree of Artaxerxes I, king of Persia (445 BC). Nehemiah's wall probably enclosed the lower city and the south-western quarter. The Temple was separately enclosed. On the north, the wall probably followed the west-east line of the present King David Street, running north of the south-western quarter and crossing the Tyropoeon Valley to meet the western wall of the Temple.

The walls of Jerusalem were repaired by the high priest Simon II about 200 BC

An overall view of the Old City of Jerusalem, from the Mount of Olives. The walls of the Old City, and the Temple Mount, can be clearly seen.

The onion-shaped domes of the Russian Church of Mary Magdalene and the Dome of the Rock, viewed from the slopes of the Mount of Olives.

'O Jerusalem, Jerusalem, you who kill the prophets . . .' (Luke 13:34)

Opposite: The Citadel viewed from outside the walls of the Old City.

Right: Part of the Citadel, built on the site of Herod's palace.

The hippodrome, part of the authentic scale model of Jerusalem in the time of Jesus.

but they were broken down in 167 BC by Antiochus Epiphanes, who built a strong citadel in the city of David, south of the Temple. The city was refortified by the Hasmonaeans, especially by John Hyrcanus (1 Maccabees 16:23).

Jerusalem was greatly beautified by Herod the Great, who erected or restored many fine buildings. Apart from the Temple, the most magnificent of all his buildings (see p. 55), he rebuilt the fortress of Baris, north-west of the Temple area, and renamed it Antonia, after his patron Mark Antony; he built a palace for himself on the west wall of the city ('Herod's palace' of Acts 23:35) and three strong towers in its neighbourhood, one of which is incorporated in the present Citadel. He also built such public installations as an amphitheatre and a hippodrome. It was under Herod, if not earlier, that a second north wall was built to enclose the north-western quarter of the city: it began at an unidentified point called the Gate Gennath and ran in a northerly and then easterly direction, passing south of the present Church of the Holy Sepulchre, until it reached the Antonia fortress. The area of the walled city that Jesus knew was about half a square mile (320 acres, or 130 hectares); its population may have been as high as 50,000. But already people were beginning to build dwelling-houses beyond the second north wall, in the section called Bezetha or Newtown; between ten and fifteen years after the death

The helmet and sword of a Roman soldier.

Remains of the pools at Bethesda (Bethzatha) – see John 5:2.

of Jesus, Herod's grandson Herod Agrippa I ('King Herod' of Acts 12:1) began to build a third north wall to enclose this suburb. After the destruction of the city by Titus in AD 70, it lay derelict for over sixty years. Then the Roman Emperor Hadrian founded a new, completely Gentile, city on the site and called it Aelia Capitolina (AD 135); the walls which enclosed it are followed substantially by the present walls of the Old City.

Some of the sites in Jerusalem mentioned in the gospel story, especially by John, can be identified with confidence; others are more doubtful. The pools of Bethesda and Siloam can be located with certainty. At Bethesda, north of the Temple area, near the present Church of St. Anne, there were twin pools which received water from a nearby source of supply. Four porticoes enclosed the area of the two pools, while a fifth

St. Anne's Church, probably the best example of Crusader architecture in Jerusalem.

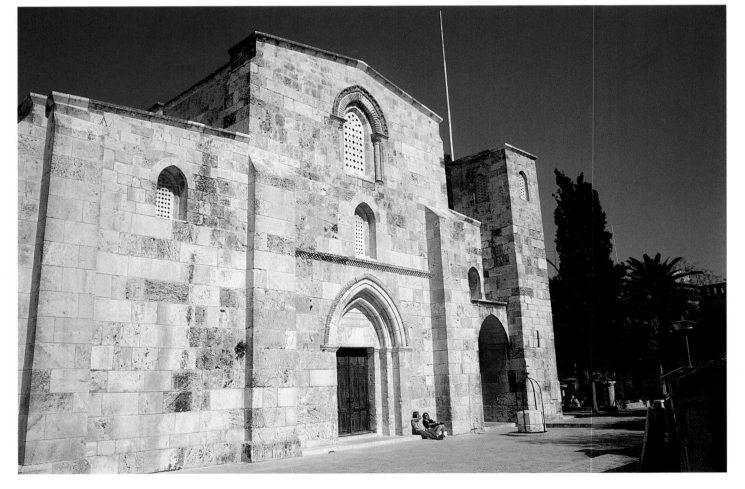

The entrance to Hezekiah's Tunnel, an important water source in ancient times.

Steps leading down to Hezekiah's Tunnel.

stood on the ridge which separated the two. The first reference to Bethesda outside the New Testament comes in the copper scroll found in Cave 3 at Qumran; it calls the place by its Hebrew name Beth-esdathain, 'the place of two outpourings'. To the water, with its reddish tinge, healing properties were ascribed, but the disabled man who had waited his turn for so long in one of the porticoes might have waited for the rest of his life if Jesus had not come along and healed him promptly and effectively (John 5:1-9).

The pool of Siloam, at the southern end of the Tyropoeon Valley, near its junction with the Valley of Hinnom (south of the city) and the Kidron Valley (east of the city), receives the water which flows through a tunnel cut through the rock from the Virgin's Fountain (the spring Gihon of the Old Testament) in the Kidron Valley, east of the city of David. The tunnel, a piece of skilled engineering work, whose construction was commemorated in a Hebrew inscription cut in the rock near its exit, is usually identified with that undertaken at the command of King Hezekiah in 701 BC (2 Kings 20:20; 2 Chronicles 32:4; Isaiah 22:9). When John reports how Jesus sent the blind man whose eyes he had smeared with clay to go to the pool of Siloam and wash it off, he mentions that Siloam means 'sent' (John 9:7). This name (Shiloah in Isaiah 8:6) referred to the 'sending' of the water from the spring Gihon through the tunnel into the pool; but John reflects that true spiritual sight is imparted only through faith in him who has been 'sent' by God.

The Mount of Olives, to the east of the city, across the Kidron, is of course an undisputed biblical site. The garden where Jesus often met with his disciples (John

Opposite: The Church of All Nations, built in 1924 on the tradional site of Jeusus' prayer in the Garden of Gethsemane.

Mosaic in the Church of St. Peter in Gallicantu – St. Peter at the Crowing of the Cock.

The Russian Church of St. Mary Magdalene and the Church of All Nations, near the site of the Garden of Gethsemane.

'Jesus began to explain . . . that he must go to Jerusalem and suffer many things . . .' (Matthew 16:21)

18:2) – called Gethsemane in the Synoptic Gospels – was on the western slope of Olivet: its location is not known for sure, but it cannot have been far from the traditional site marked by the Church of All Nations and other commemorative buildings. The Franciscans maintain a garden in the immediate vicinity; some of the olives in it may be up to 1,000 years old. The Church of Eleona (i.e. Olivet) was built by Constantine on the summit of the hill to enclose a cave where Jesus was believed to have instructed the inner circle of his disciples. The Bordeaux pilgrim saw the church when he visited Palestine in AD 333. This was also the first place where the ascension of Jesus was commemorated by Christians. But about AD 390 a noble lady named Poemenia founded a colonnade a little way off, called the Holy Ascension, surrounding the rock from which some believed Jesus to have ascended into heaven. On this site there now stands a circular domed building. It is under Muslim guardianship, but Christians are permitted to hold an Ascension Day service there. The rock is still to be seen inside the building; the custodians point out a depression in it – in shape not

'They came to place called Golgotha . . .' (Mathew 27:33)

Christian pilgrims throng the Via Dolorosa on Good Friday.

unlike a human footprint, which they say was made by one of Jesus' feet immediately before he ascended.

No great certainty attaches to some of the sites recalling episodes in the passion narrative, such as the Cenacle (the house where the Last Supper was eaten) or the Church of St. Peter in Gallicantu, said to stand where the high priest's palace stood. For the place where Jesus appeared before Pilate there are two rival sites. The place is called the Praetorium in Mark 15:16; this word denotes the headquarters of the governor or commanding officer, and in the context of the trial narrative it might refer either to the Antonia fortress or to Herod's palace. Beneath the Convent of the Sisters of Zion, which stands more or less where the Antonia fortress did, may be seen a Roman pavement which has been identified with the Pavement of John 19:13, where Pilate pronounced judgement on Jesus. The lines of the soldiers' 'game of the king' are traced out on one part of the pavement; this, it is suggested, may be the very spot where they dressed Jesus up in mock-royal robes and hailed him as King of the Jews. In the opinion of some reputable archaeologists, however, this pavement, like the Ecce Homo arch visible in the street above, dates back only to Hadrian's time. If the Antonia fortress was indeed the Praetorium of the Gospels. then the present line of the Via Dolorosa corresponds more or less to the actual road on which Jesus was led to the cross – only several feet higher. If the Praetorium was Herod's palace, then the actual way to the cross must have been quite different from the traditional one.

The place of crucifixion was outside the city gate (Hebrews 13:12). The Church of the Holy Sepulchre, which traditionally marks the site of Jesus' death, burial and resurrection, stood just outside the second north wall. The memory of the site was preserved even after Hadrian had enclosed it within his own north wall and erected a

The Fifth Station along the Via Dolorosa marks the place where, by tradition, Simon of Cyrene took up the cross.

The Church of the Holy Sepulchre, Jerusalem.

pagan temple there. It was because of the persistence of the Christian tradition that Constantine about AD 325, removed the pagan installations and brought to light the holy sepulchre. The Bordeaux pilgrim visited the place while Constantine's basilica was being built, and mentions the rock outcrop called Golgotha, 'where the Lord was crucified, and about a stone's throw from it the vault where they laid his body and from which he rose again on the third day'. Constantine's basilica, the Church of the Holy Sepulchre (consecrated about AD 335), was originally and more happily called the Anastasis or 'Resurrection' (it was so called by Egeria fifty years after its consecration).

It calls for a powerful effort of the imagination for the visitor to the church today to envisage the site as it was in Jesus' time. Many visitors get a better impression of what it looked like from the Garden Tomb, off the Nablus road. Here we have a garden containing a tomb, like that described in John 19:41, although it cannot be seriously claimed that this is the historical site. The suggestion that it was so goes back to 1883, when the identification formed part of General Gordon's fancy that

The Church of the Holy Sepulchre, Jerusalem.

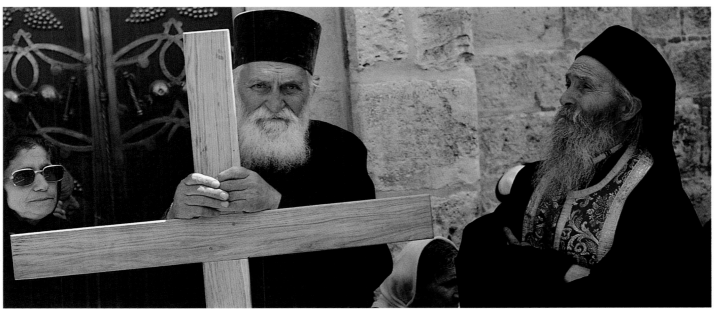

Good Friday in the Old City, Jerusalem.

The Garden Tomb, a haven of peace, just outside the Damascus Gate.

Jerusalem was laid out on the plan of a human body, with Calvary or Golgotha, 'the place of a skull', corresponding to the head. It is sufficient to reflect that, whatever place is pointed out as Jesus' tomb, 'he is not here, for he has risen'.

Akeldama – by tradition the place where Judas Iscariot hanged himself.

What makes a city 'holy'?

In Matthew 4:5 Jerusalem is called 'the holy city'; yet in Matthew 23:37 it is charged with killing the prophets and stoning those sent to it. In Matthew 5:35 it is 'the city of the Great King'; in Revelation 11:8 it is 'the great city, which is figuratively called Sodom and Egypt, where also their Lord was crucified'.

A strange set of contradictions, one might think. What really makes a city holy?

The Temple

A Jewish coin with the only known contemporary depiction of Herod's Temple.

When Jesus had completed his journey on Palm Sunday, he 'entered Jerusalem and went to the Temple. He looked around at everything, but since it was already late, he went out to Bethany with the Twelve' (Mark 11:11).

The Temple Jesus knew was the Temple renovated, enlarged and beautified by Herod the Great. Architecturally it was new: religiously it was still Zerubbabel's Temple, rebuilt after the Jews returned from the Babylonian exile. The six centuries between the return from exile and the destruction of Jerusalem in AD 70 are known in Jewish history as the age of the Second Temple.

The site on which the Temple stood had sacred associations reaching back to ancient times: according to tradition, the rock which crops out on the top of the Temple hill was the place where Abraham built the altar to sacrifice Isaac – one of the mountains in 'the region of Moriah' (Genesis 22:2) being identified with 'Mount Moriah' (2 Chronicles 3:1).

Solomon's Temple had stood on the site for over 350 years when it was destroyed by the Babylonians (587 BC) beyond the possibility of repair. About seventy years later a completely new Temple was built there, by authorisation of the Persian king. When it was dedicated on March 12, 515 BC, some very old people who could remember Solomon's Temple reckoned it a poor thing in comparison with its magnificent predecessor. Yet the contemporary prophet Haggai predicted far greater glory for it in days to come (Haggai 2:3-9). The high priesthood in the new Temple remained for nearly 350 years in the family of Zadok, which had supplied the chief priests in Solomon's Temple from its dedication onwards.

The Temple was repaired, extended and adorned at various times between Zerubbabel and Herod. One man who is credited with a distinguished contribution to this work is Simon II, high priest about 200 BC: among other things, he fortified the Temple precincts with a surrounding wall. A few decades after his time the Temple suffered a major – but, mercifully, short-lived – disaster when, in the days of the Maccabees, it was turned over by the persecuting king Antiochus Epiphanes to the worship of a pagan deity, scornfully referred to by the Jews as 'the abomination of desolation' (1 Maccabees 1:54). This desecration lasted for exactly three years: the regaining and re-consecration of the Temple by Judas Maccabaeus in December 164 BC, has been commemorated ever since by Hanukkah, the Jewish Feast of Dedication. In John 10:22 Jesus is said to have walked in the Temple courts during this feast less than four months before his death.

The sanctuary of Herod's Temple, from the authentic scale model of Jerusalem in the time of Christ.

Opposite:
Wilson's Arch
originally
supported a
magnificent
stairway leading
to Herod's
Temple.

None of the restorations or extensions of the second Temple could match, however, with the work initiated by Herod at the beginning of 19 BC. Because certain parts of the building could not be entered by the laity, a thousand Levites were specially trained as builders and masons, and carried out their work so efficiently and carefully that at no time was there any interruption in the sacrifices and other services. The Temple platform was extended eastwards on vaulted foundations, with strong retaining walls, so as to increase the area of the precincts, especially of the outer court. The courts were enclosed by magnificent colonnades. Along the east side of the outer court ran what was called Solomon's Colonnade; it was here that Jesus was seen walking during the Feast of the Dedication. Before long it became a habitual meeting place for the infant church

The triple arches of the original gateways into Herod's Temple may be discerned in the walls surrounding the Temple Mount.

(see Acts 3:11; 5:12).

Wealthy Jews of the dispersion (that is, those living outside Palestine) sent costly offerings to enhance the splendour of the place. For example, the gate called Beautiful of Acts 3:2, 10 is generally identified with the magnificent gate of Corinthian bronze presented by an Alexandrian Jew named Nicanor (after whom it is also called the Nicanor Gate). It

probably stood at the top of the steps leading up from the outer court to the Court of the Women.

While the main part of Herod's rebuilding was completed before his death in 4 BC, the work went on for more than sixty years after that. When Jesus visited the Temple at the first Passover of his ministry it was remarked that the place had by then been forty-six years under

The Temple precincts, from the Holy Land Hotel model of Jerusalem

'What massive stones! What magnificent buildings!' (Mark 13:1)

construction. The work was not entirely finished until AD 63, only seven years before the destruction of the whole fabric.

We are fortunate in having an eyewitness account of Herod's Temple from Josephus, who was born into a priestly family of Jerusalem in AD 37. He was thus well acquainted with the Temple in the days of its greatest architectural glory and was present with the Roman forces when it was burned in AD 70. Another detailed description, preserved in the tradition of the rabbinical schools, was finally set down in writing about AD 200, in a tractate of the *Mishnah* (the authoritative compilation of Jewish oral law) called *Middoth* ('measurements').

The whole area was holy, but it became increasingly holy as one penetrated farther in, from east to west. The outer court, enclosed by Herod with colonnades, is sometimes referred to as the Court of the Gentiles because non-Jews (like the Greeks of John 12:20) were permitted to enter it and walk about in it. But they were forbidden to go into any of the inner courts: notices in Greek and Latin gave warning that the penalty for such trespass was death. The Romans permitted the Jewish authorities to pass the death-sentence for this offence and to carry it out even if the offender were a Roman citizen. It was for allegedly aiding and abetting an offence of this kind that Paul was attacked and nearly beaten to death by an angry crowd during his last visit to Jerusalem (Acts 21:27-32).

The inner courts were on a

Opposite: The Temple Mount is today dominated by the Dome of the Rock.

Left: The Dome of the Winds, on the Temple Mount.

Bottom: Islamic architecture dominates the Temple Mount area.

higher level than the outer court: one had to go up several steps to get into them. The easternmost of the inner courts was the Court of the Women – so called because Jewish women were admitted thus far (but no farther). In this court, at the west end, was the 'treasury', the section where there stood thirteen trumpet-shaped containers for voluntary offerings of money. Jesus was sitting 'opposite the place where the offerings were put' when he saw the widow put into one of the containers the two 'very small copper coins' which were all that she had (Mark 12:41-44).

Beyond that was the Court of Israel, which was open to Jewish laymen. The innermost court was the Court of the Priests, normally barred to all laymen. In the eastern part of this court, opposite the main gates leading from the other courts and the eastern entrance into the Temple precincts, so that it could be seen from a distance, stood the great altar of burnt-offering. At its west side stood the sanctuary proper, comprising (from east to west) the porch, the holy

place and the cubical holy of holies. Into the holy place the priests entered to discharge various duties, in particular to offer incense on the golden incense-altar, as Zechariah did on the occasion when an angel appeared to him and announced the forthcoming birth of his son John the Baptist (Luke 1:8-23). No ordinary priest could hope that the lot for offering the incense would fall to him on more than one day in his lifetime (if that); the day when Zechariah received the angelic announcement was in any case the red-letter day of his whole priestly career. Into the holy of holies only the high priest was allowed to go,

and that but once a year, on the Day of Atonement in the autumn, when he presented sacrificial blood to expiate his own sins and those of the nation which he represented (Leviticus 16:1-4). In the Letter to the Hebrews this ritual is used as a parable (by contrast more than by comparison) of Jesus' atoning death and his present high-priestly ministry in the heavenly sanctuary. But during his Palestinian ministry Jesus, as a layman, could not go beyond the Court of Israel: 'if he were on earth, he would not be a priest' (Hebrews 8:4).

Herod's Temple and its precincts covered an area of twenty-six acres (ten and a

The Western Wall, often known as the Wailing Wall, is a spot revered by Jews, as its stones date back to Herod's Temple.

An Arab funeral at the El Aqsa Mosque on the Temple Mount.

half hectares). (The Haram Es-Sharif, or 'Noble Enclosure', which occupies the same site today, covers thirty-five acres – just over fourteen hectares.) The walls surrounding the area provided it with a system of fortification quite distinct from that of the city. Part of Herod's walls, built of the huge stones which characterised his work, may be seen today: the most famous part is the Western Wall (formerly known as the Wailing Wall), the most sacred place of prayer in the Jewish world. The walls were pierced by several gates: there were four on the Western Wall, leading down into the Tyropoeon Valley (see p. 44). From the Western Wall also a viaduct was carried on arches across the valley to the upper city on the west: the pier of the easternmost arch is still to be seen springing from the Western Wall (it is known as Wilson's Arch, after Sir Charles Wilson, a British archaeologist of the nineteenth century). Farther south the remains of another arch can be seen springing from the Western Wall: this arch (Robinson's Arch, after the American pioneer explorer Edward Robinson) carried the first stage of a staircase which then turned south and led down to the main street. The staircase connected at the top with the Royal Colonnade or Royal Stoa, a covered gallery running along the whole southern side of the outer court and described by Josephus as a structure 'more noteworthy than any other under the sun'.

Jesus' first contact with the Temple was in his early infancy, when he was taken there for the ceremony of purification and was hailed as the coming Deliverer by Simeon and Anna (Luke 2:22-38). His next recorded visit to it was at the age of twelve, when – perhaps to prepare him for his Bar Mitzvah confirmation the following year he was taken there at Passover time by Mary and Joseph and was found in conversation with the rabbis who had their 'teaching pitches' in the outer court (Luke 2:41-51).

The day was to come when Jesus himself, on successive visits to Jerusalem, would be a familiar figure as he taught in the outer court. Several of his discourses reported in the Gospel of John were delivered there – possibly the discourse on resurrection and judgement which followed the healing of the man at the pool of Bethesda (John 5:19-47) and certainly the discourses at the Feast of Tabernacles (John 7:14–8:58), at the Feast of Dedication (John 10:22-39) and during the week before the last Passover (John 12:30-36, 44-50).

It is there that the scene of the adulterous woman is set (John 8:2-11). It was there, too, that a challenge to Jesus' authority was answered with his parable of the vineyard, and that he dealt with the question about paying tribute to Caesar, refuted the Sadducees' objection against the doctrine of resurrection, gave a ruling on the two great commandments of the law and asked the scribes how the Messiah, being David's lord, could be his son (Mark 11:27–12:37).

Jesus' cleansing of the Temple is recorded in all four Gospels. John, perhaps because its implication for the replacement of the old order by a new one entitled it to a position in the forefront of Jesus' ministry, puts it in the context of an earlier visit to Jerusalem than the Synoptists do (compare John 2:13-22 with Matthew 21:12,13; Mark 11:15-18; Luke 19:45,46). It was in a section of the outer court that the vendors of sacrificial animals and the money-changers had set up their stalls and tables, and by doing so they encroached on its proper use. The outer court was the only part of the Temple area where Gentiles could draw near to the God of Israel; Jesus' action made more room for them, and his quotation of Isaiah 56:7, 'My house shall be called a house of prayer for all nations' (Mark 11:17), suggests that he had their interests in mind. Those Greeks who had come to Jerusalem to worship God at the last Passover may have asked to see Jesus because they recognised that he had championed their spiritual interests (John 12:21).

The cleansing of the Temple was not the signal for a popular rising, although the Jewish authorities feared it might lead to that. It was rather a symbolical action like those sometimes performed by the Old Testament prophets to confirm their

The Old City and Dome of the Rock at night, from the Mount of Olives.

words. It is evident that no breach of the peace was involved, for there was no intervention by the Roman soldiers stationed in the adjoining Antonia fortress, north-west of the Temple area, which communicated with the outer court by two flights of steps (compare Acts 21:35,40).

Jesus' last utterance about the Temple foretold its downfall. His disciples had been impressed by the magnificence of the structure, but as he sat with some of them on the slope of the Mount of Olives, looking across to the Temple area, he spoke of the time, not more than a generation distant, when not one stone would be left standing on another (Mark 13:2-30).

When Jesus was on trial before the high priest, an attempt was made to convict him of speaking against the Temple, but it failed because the witnesses gave conflicting evidence. Even so, people remembered what he was charged with saying, and when he was on the cross some passers-by mocked him as the one 'who was going to destroy the temple and build it in three days' (Mark 15:29). 'But,' says John, the only evangelist who reports him as actually using such language, 'the temple was his body' (John 2:21).

At the moment of Jesus' death, we are told, 'the curtain of the temple was torn in two from top to bottom' (Mark 15:38). If this was the curtain that hung before the holy of holies, the throne-room of the invisible presence of God, the incident seems to show that in the death of Jesus, God is fully revealed.

Cleansing the Temple

'The Lord you are seeking will come to his temple' (Malachi 3:1). Many interpreters, especially in earlier days, have found the fulfilment of this prophecy in Jesus' cleansing of the Temple. Do you think this is likely? Consider the refining and purifying work which, in Malachi's prophecy, the Lord will undertake when he visits his Temple. Could Jesus' cleansing be described in these terms?

Jesus reminds his hearers how Isaiah had spoken of the Temple as 'a house of prayer for all nations' (Mark 11:17). But that Temple had long since disappeared; is there anything to which the same description could be applied today?

Index